DALE EARNHARDT JR.:
Tragedy and Triumph

BY JIM GIGLIOTTI

TRADITION BOOKS®
A New Tradition in Children's Publishing™
MAPLE PLAIN, MINNESOTA

Published by **Tradition Books**® and distributed to the school and library market by **The Child's World**®
P.O. Box 326
Chanhassen, MN 55317-0326
800/599-READ
http://www.childsworld.com

Photo Credits
Cover: Sports Gallery/Al Messerschmidt (2).
Allsport/Robert Laberge: 14, 15
AP/Wide World: 5, 18, 19, 20, 21
Corbis: 6, 10, 17
Sports Gallery: 9, 26, 27 (Al Messerschmidt), 8 (Brian Cleary), 23, 24, 28 (Joe Robbins); 11, 13 (Brian Spurlock)

An Editorial Directions book
Editorial Directions, Inc.: E. Russell Primm, Editorial Director; Katie Marsico and Elizabeth K. Martin, Assistant Editors; Olivia Nellums, Editorial Assistant; Susan Hindman, Copy Editor; Susan Ashley, Proofreader; Kevin Cunningham, Fact Checker; Tim Griffin/IndexServ, Indexer; James Buckley Jr., Photo Researcher and Selector

The Design Lab: Kathy Petelinsek, Art Director and Designer; Kari Thornborough, Page Production

Library of Congress Cataloging-in-Publication Data
Gigliotti, Jim.
  Dale Earnhardt, Jr. : tragedy and triumph / by Jim Gigliotti.
    p. cm. — (The world of NASCAR)
"An Editorial Directions book"—T.p. verso.
Summary: A biography of the NASCAR driver who is the son of another winning racecar driver, Dale Earnhardt, Sr. Includes bibliographical references and index.
  ISBN 1-59187-027-5 (lib. bdg. : alk. paper)
  1. Earnhardt, Dale, Jr.—Juvenile literature. 2. Automobile racing drivers—United States—Biography—Juvenile literature. [1. Earnhardt, Dale, Jr. 2. Automobile racing drivers.]
I. Title. II. Series.
GV1032.E19 G54 2004 796.72'092—dc21   2003008447

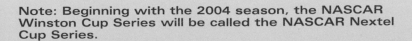

Note: Beginning with the 2004 season, the NASCAR Winston Cup Series will be called the NASCAR Nextel Cup Series.

D A L E   E A R N H A R D T   J R .

Table of Contents

INTRODUCTION

"We'll Get through This"

S hortly after the Daytona 500 in February 2001, NASCAR president Mike Helton delivered shocking news. "We've lost Dale Earnhardt," he said.

Earnhardt was one of the most respected drivers in the history of **NASCAR.** He also was one of the most successful. He won a record-tying seven Winston Cup championships as NASCAR's best driver over the course of a season. But in the final turn on the final lap of this Daytona 500, Earnhardt crashed his famous No. 3 car. He died at the hospital a short time later.

The news was devastating to NASCAR fans. To many of them, Earnhardt was a legend. He was an icon of the sport.

Those fans lost a hero. Dale Earnhardt Jr. lost a hero, too, but he lost much more than that. He lost his father. "The key to all my success is my dad," Dale Jr. once told *Sports Illustrated.* "It's that simple. He taught me how to drive, how to live with **integrity,** and how to be a man."

One week after his father's fatal accident, Dale Jr. was back on the racetrack. He and his crew believed that is what

A week after his father's death, Dale Earnhardt Jr. listens as other drivers speak about the NASCAR legend.

Dale Sr. would have wanted. "We'll get through this," Dale Jr. said at the time. The younger Earnhardt clearly wasn't himself, though, as he struggled through a number of races. Then in July, less than five months after his father's death, Dale Jr. won the Pepsi 400. It came at Daytona. Dale Jr.'s road had taken him from tragedy to triumph.

An emotional victory: Dale holds up his winning trophy from the 2001 Pepsi 400 at Daytona.

CHAPTER ONE

A Family Affair

The Earnhardt family has had a long association with NASCAR. Dale Earnhardt Jr.'s grandfather was Ralph Earnhardt, a member of the International Motorsports Hall of Fame. He was named one of the 50 greatest drivers in NASCAR history when the organization celebrated its 50-year anniversary in 1998. Ralph's son Dale Earnhardt Sr. also made the list.

Ralph Earnhardt was a hugely successful driver in the 1950s and 1960s. He won more than 350 NASCAR races of all different classifications. In those days, however, stock-car racing was more of a **regional** sport enjoyed in the Southeast. Ralph generally raced close to his family's North Carolina home, often on Friday and Saturday nights. Many times, Ralph's son Dale accompanied his father to the track and helped him out in the garage at home. That fueled Dale's passion for racing. He wanted to be just like dad.

In 1974, Dale Jr. was born. By the time he was old enough to hang out at the track, NASCAR was no longer just a regional sport. It was becoming a national obsession, and Dale Sr. was one of its most famous drivers. Racing usually took place on Sundays and in cities all over the United States. That meant that Dale Sr. often had a plane to catch

Dale Earnhardt Sr. was known as the "Man in Black" for the paint color of his famous No. 3 car.

or a sponsor to call upon or an interview to do. "I was working and racing and going all the time," the elder Earnhardt used to say.

While Dale Jr. didn't get to hang out with his dad as much as he would have liked, it made the time they did have together all the more special. One month after his dad's fatal accident, Dale Jr. shared some of those memories in a column he wrote for NASCAR.com. "Since his death, these are the memories that help me through the hard times," Dale Jr. told his fans.

Dale Sr. is one of only two drivers who have won seven NASCAR championships.

He wrote about his dad teaching him how to ski when he was six years old. He wrote about a middle-of-the-night road trip when he got to tag along with his dad and some of his friends. Of course, there were racing memories, too, such as advice his father gave him when he first joined the NASCAR circuit.

Like any son, Dale Jr. didn't always understand or appreciate the advice. And like any son, he always strived for his father's approval. "It's like a never-ending process earning his respect," Dale Jr. once told the *Charlotte Observer.* "It's bottomless. . . . But it's something you always want."

Dale Jr. and Dale Sr. continued a NASCAR family tradition as old as NASCAR itself.

EIGHT IS ENOUGH

Dale Earnhardt Jr. drives the No. 8 car in Winston Cup races. That was the number that Dale Jr.'s grandfather, Ralph Earnhardt, drove.

Dale Jr. never knew his grandfather. Ralph died of a heart attack at the age of 45 while working on his car in 1973. Dale Jr. was born the next year. Dale Sr., however, instilled in his son a deep appreciation for the family's racing history. "I'm proud of my father and my grandfather and what they've done," Dale Jr. says.

After his father's death, there was talk about Dale Jr. switching to No. 3. He knows he's already carrying on a family tradition with the No. 8, though. "My father did a lot for the number three," Dale Jr. says. "But the number eight has more significance for us."

Owner Richard Childress still has the rights to No. 3, which Dale Jr. raced in some Busch series events in 2002. In fact, Dale Jr. won in No. 3 in a Busch race at Daytona.

In a Busch race in 2002, Dale Jr. wore the family's most famous number on his car.

C H A P T E R   T W O

Rising Star

As a youngster, Dale Jr. raced **go-karts.** He didn't necessarily aspire to follow in his dad's footsteps, however, until 1991. That year, he and his half-brother Kerry bought a late-model stock car. Dale Jr. was 17 years old, and he decided to pursue a racing career.

Once he began racing seriously, he was an immediate success. He started out by competing in the street stock division at the Concord, North Carolina, Speedway. Next came the NASCAR Late Model/Stock Division. By 1997, when he was only 22 years old, he already was competing regularly in NASCAR Busch Series races. The Busch Series is one step down from the Winston Cup Series, like the highest minor leagues in baseball. Busch Series cars are a bit lighter than, and not as powerful as, Winston Cup cars.

Dale Jr. took the Busch Series by storm. He placed 14th in his first event and needed only 16 starts before he recorded his first victory. The win came in the Coca-Cola 300 at Fort Worth, Texas, in April 1998. He won in true Earnhardt fashion, with a bold move to pass the leader on the last lap. Dale Sr. was on the radio during the race, helping to coach his son. "He used his head all day and ran a great race," an emotional Dale Sr. said afterward. "I couldn't be more proud of him."

There were many more chances for Dale Sr. to be proud. Dale Jr. went on to win six more races that year. He placed among the top five finishers nine other times. By season's end, he edged Matt Kenseth for the Busch Series title.

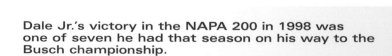

Dale Jr.'s victory in the NAPA 200 in 1998 was one of seven he had that season on his way to the Busch championship.

The next year was more of the same. Dale Jr. won six races and again was the Busch Series champion. He also got his feet wet in the Winston Cup by racing in five series events. He was ready to be a full-time driver in the Winston Cup Series.

In April 2000, Dale Jr. won his first Winston Cup race. It came almost two years to the day after he won his first Busch Series race, and it came at the same site. Dale Jr. won the DIRECTV 500 at the Texas Motor Speedway. Later, Dale Jr. added a victory in the Pontiac Excitement 400 at Richmond International Speedway.

Dale Jr.'s bright red No. 8 car paced the field in his first NASCAR victory in 2000 at the Texas Motor Speedway.

Dale Jr.'s most memorable moment, though, came when he won The Winston at Charlotte in May. The Winston doesn't count in NASCAR's point standings. It's an all-star race. No **rookie** ever had won it before. That's not what made the win so special, though. What made it special was that Dale Jr.'s dad was there to share it with him. Dale Sr. joined his son in the winner's circle, and the two celebrated together. Dale Sr. didn't have a plane to catch or another race to go to, so "we jumped around and hollered and just made fools of ourselves," Dale Jr. says. "It was the happiest time I think I ever spent with my dad. I felt like I had really done something. . . . I knew Dad felt the same way."

At the Winston in 2000, under the lights at Charlotte, Dale Jr. became the first rookie to win the event.

FAMILY FEUD

Dale Jr. and his brother Kerry made history when they joined their father in the same Winston Cup race in 2000. In August that year, the three Earnhardts raced together in the Pepsi 400 at Michigan International Speedway.

Dad got the better of the competition. Dale Jr. qualified with the best time and sat on the pole, but finished 31st. Kerry spun out on the fifth lap and finished last. Dale Sr. started out near the back of the pack but finished sixth.

The only other time two brothers competed against their father was in 1960. That year, brothers Richard and Maurice Petty raced against their dad, Lee.

Kerry Earnhardt added to the family legacy by joining brother Dale and father Dale in a 2000 Winston Cup race.

CHAPTER THREE

Agony and Ecstasy

D ale Jr. had tremendous success as a rookie in 2000. He won three races, including the Winston, and finished 16th in the Winston Cup standings. He was disappointed, though, that he was not the top rookie on the NASCAR circuit. That distinction went to his friend Matt Kenseth, who finished 14th in the standings. So Dale Jr. entered the 2001 season determined to make it an even better year. He wanted to get the season off to a fast start at the Daytona 500.

Each NASCAR season begins with the Daytona 500. It's the most famous and the most prestigious event on the schedule. Every NASCAR driver dreams of crossing the finish line first at Daytona. In Dale Jr.'s case, the dream was literal. In the weeks before the 2001 Daytona 500, he had a recurring dream when he slept. It was **vivid.** "I'm pretty confident that I'm going to

win the Daytona 500," he told the media a few days before the race, "because I've dreamed about it so much."

Late in the race, Dale Jr. had a chance to make that dream come true. Unfortunately, it turned into a nightmare. Dale Jr. was running in second place, just ahead of Dale Sr. and just behind Michael Waltrip. Dale Sr. raced for Richard Childress Racing Enterprises, Inc., and Dale Jr. and Waltrip raced for Dale Earnhardt, Inc. When it was apparent that Dale Sr. was not going to win the race, he decided to run interference for his son and Waltrip. No one was going to get past him and deny victory for either Waltrip or Dale Jr.

As it turned out, Waltrip held off Dale Jr. to win for the first

Ken Schrader's car plows into Dale Earnhardt Sr.'s at the 2001 Daytona 500. Sadly, Dale Sr. died as a result of the crash.

time in his Winston Cup career. The celebration in Victory Circle didn't last long, however. Word came quickly that Dale Sr. was hurt badly when his car slammed headfirst into the wall on the final turn. A short time later, NASCAR officials confirmed the worst: Dale Sr. had died.

After much soul-searching, Dale Jr. and his crew decided to race the following weekend at the Dura Lube 400 in Rockingham, North Carolina. "I'm sure he'd want us to keep going, and that's what we're going to do," Dale Jr. said. On the very first lap, Dale Jr. crashed. It was a horrifying moment for family and friends who were still reeling from Dale Sr.'s crash. Luckily, Dale Jr. walked away from the wreck uninjured. He vowed to try again

NASCAR fans everywhere were stunned by Dale Sr.'s death. Many left flowers and tributes at tracks around the nation.

the following week in Las Vegas.

Things went better at the UAW-DaimlerChrysler 400 in Las Vegas, but Dale Jr. still finished a distant 23rd. It was not until he returned to Daytona in July that he broke into the winner's circle again. He won the Pepsi 400 by holding off Waltrip on the final lap. Dale Jr. immediately dedicated the emotional victory to his dad. "He was with me tonight," he said after the race.

Dale Jr. says that returning to Daytona helped him with his father's death. It's no coincidence that his racing improved. He won two more times in 2001. By season's end, he had ascended to eighth place in the Winston Cup standings.

Dale Jr. takes the checkered flag at the Pepsi 400 at Daytona, just five months after his father's crash on the same track.

FAST TRACK

It is ironic that the site of Dale Earnhardt Jr.'s greatest sorrow also has been the site of some of his greatest joys. Dale Jr. has been enormously successful at Daytona International Speedway in Daytona Beach, Florida.

"I really like this racetrack," Dale Jr. said after winning the EAS/GNC Live Well 300 in February 2002. It was his sixth consecutive race at Daytona in which he finished first or second. "If I could run here every week, I would. It's the most perfectly built racetrack I've ever been on."

Dale Jr.'s win at the historic track came as part of a deal in which he returned to the Busch Series for three races in 2002. He raced as the No. 3 car, the car his father made famous. Dale Jr. also won at Daytona in his first race there after his father's death. Dale Sr. holds the Daytona record with 34 career victories.

"Number three is back in Victory Lane!" Dale Jr. shouted after the EAS/GNC Live Well 300. "I know my daddy would be real happy."

Dale has had a lot of success on the Daytona track. Here he shows off his 2002 Gatorade 125 race trophy.

C H A P T E R   F O U R

A Name for Himself

With the emotional roller coaster of the 2001 season behind him, Dale Jr. entered 2002 with renewed enthusiasm. He began the season strong. He was in fifth place in the standings after winning the Aaron's 499 at Talladega Superspeedway in Alabama in April. An accident the next week, however, left him with a **concussion.** He fell to 16th in the standings over the next few months.

Still, Dale Jr. **rebounded** from the injury to finish the season in 11th place. He won another race, the EA Sports 500, at Talladega in October. It was one of five consecutive top 10 finishes late in the year. "We'll go out strong," he said late in the 2002 season. "We'll do what we can to convince all of those people who picked us as championship contenders this year that we're going to be the ones to beat next year."

Wearing a snappy cowboy hat, a smiling Dale poses with his trophy after winning the 2002 Aaron's 499 race.

Dale Jr. has a lot of good things to look forward to in his NASCAR career. He's off to a roaring start!

Dale Jr. turned 29 during the 2003 season. Dale Sr. won his first Winston Cup at age 29 in 1980. For the younger Earnhardt, the comparisons between father and son have been **inevitable** throughout his career. "I never told anybody that I was going to be as good as my dad," he told *The Sporting News*. "I've read that a lot, and I appreciate the comparisons, but that has a backlash when you don't run well every week. I just want to drive race cars and make a living doing it."

With career earnings of more than $10 million already, he's made a pretty good living doing it. Few people doubt that Dale Jr. will eventually be a Winston Cup champion, perhaps even in 2003. "Junior's on his way to the championship," fellow driver Robby Gordon told NASCAR.com late in the 2002 season. "He hasn't done as well as he'd have liked this year, but he's still the most popular guy out there."

Indeed, Dale Jr. draws huge crowds of fans wherever he goes. At first, he was known simply as the son of Dale Sr.

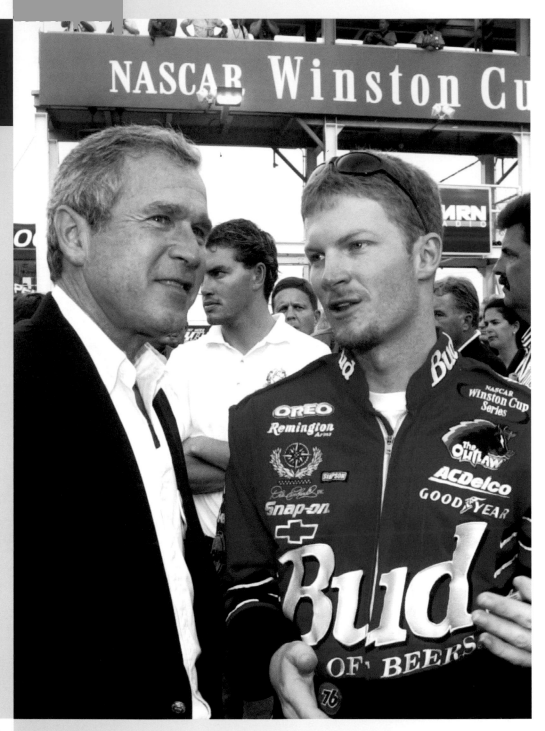

George Bush was the governor of Texas when he met with Dale Jr. before a race in 2000 in Texas.

Even his nickname, Little E, reflected that. Now he is known as one of the hottest stars on the NASCAR circuit. He's on talk shows and in commercials. His pit area is frequented by celebrities and models. Music television stations such as MTV and VH-1 scramble to get him on their shows. He gets as much attention as the music stars he idolizes.

All that doesn't **detract** from Dale Jr.'s main focus, though: winning. In that sense, Little E really is just like his dad. "I just want to win," Dale Jr. told NASCAR.com. "I want to win championships. Nothing else really matters."

Lookin' good: Dale has a lot of fun, but he knows that driving is a serious business.

NORMAL GUY

Dale Earnhardt Jr. is not your father's NASCAR star. He is part of a young corps of drivers on the circuit, along with the likes of Ryan Newman and Matt Kenseth. But Dale Jr. is a breed unto himself. He tells stories about hanging out with rock stars and partying all night at his North Carolina home. He counts music heavyweights such as Kid Rock and Sheryl Crow among his friends. He was a presenter at the 2001 MTV Awards. People magazine has named him one of the world's "Sexiest Men" and "Most Intriguing People."

Dale Jr., though, has remained remarkably unaffected by all the attention. He sees himself as the same person he was before NASCAR fame hit. His greatest pleasures are the simple ones. A bachelor, he likes "chillin' with his friends" and playing computer games.

"I don't see myself, I guess, like a lot of people do," Dale Jr. told WFNZ Radio in Charlotte, North Carolina. "I still see myself as the same guy I was ten years ago."

Dale's fans crowd into the pit area to get a close-up look at their hero's car.

DALE EARNHARDT JR.'S LIFE

1974 Dale Earnhardt Jr. born on October 10 in Kannapolis, North Carolina

1991 Begins professional racing career in Concord, North Carolina

1996 Finishes 13th in first Busch Series race in Myrtle Beach, South Carolina

1998 Takes the checkered flag at the Coca-Cola 300 for his first Busch Series victory; wins six more Busch Series races and the overall points title

1999 Debuts in the Winston Cup with a 16th-place finish at the Coca-Cola 600; makes it back-to-back Busch championships after winning six races

2000 In only his 12th Winston Cup start, he wins the DIRECTV 500; competes against brother Kerry and father Dale Sr. in a Winston Cup race in Michigan; finishes 16th in the Winston Cup standings, second best among rookies

2001 Wins the Pepsi 400 in his first race at Daytona following his father's death there; earns first top 10 finish in Winston Cup standings when he places eighth

2002 Races in his father's No. 3 and wins Busch Series event at Daytona; finishes 11th in the Winston Cup standings in his third season on the circuit

GLOSSARY

concussion—an injury, usually to the brain, that results from a jarring hit and temporarily affects the ability of a person to function properly

detract—take away or reduce in importance

go-karts—small, open, four-wheel racers with gasoline engines

inevitable—impossible to avoid

integrity—maintaining personal beliefs or a code of living

NASCAR—the National Association for Stock Car Automobile Racing

rebounded—recovered or regained health

regional—relating to a particular area of the country

rookie—a driver in his first year at a given level of racing

vivid—clear and distinct, lifelike

FOR MORE INFORMATION ABOUT DALE EARNHARDT JR.

Books

Barber, Phil. *Dale Earnhardt: The Likeable Intimidator.* Excelsior, Minn.: Tradition Books, 2002.

Earnhardt Jr., Dale. *Driver #8.* New York: Warner Books, 2002.

Kirkpatrick, Rob. *Dale Earnhardt Jr.: NASCAR Road Racer.* New York: PowerKids Press, 2000.

Persinger, Kathy. *Dale Earnhardt Jr.: Born to Race.* Sports Publishing, Inc., 2001.

Stewart, Mark. *Dale Earnhardt Jr.: Driven by Destiny.* Brookfield, Conn.: Millbrook Press, 2003.

Web Sites

CNNSI.com
http://sportsillustrated.cnn.com
For motorsports news, racing results, and commentary, click on NASCAR

Dale Earnhardt Jr.'s Official Site
http://www.dalejr.com
To visit Dale Earnhardt Jr.'s official site for photos, news updates, and to send e-mail to the driver and his team

The Official Web Site of NASCAR
http://www.nascar.com
For an overview of each season of NASCAR, as well as the history of the sport, statistics, and a dictionary of racing terms

INDEX

ABOUT THE AUTHOR

Jim Gigliotti is a freelance writer who lives with his wife and two children in Westlake Village, California. He has worked for the University of Southern California athletic department, the Los Angeles Dodgers, and the National Football League. He previously wrote about NASCAR stars Jeff Gordon and Dale Jarrett.